The Report On Sales

Contents

Introduction

Those of you familiar with my work know I have been publishing an award winning blog on sales, called The Pipeline, (http://sellbetter.ca/blog), since 2007. Over the years my pieces were picked up here and there, mainstream and wide-stream media. Late in 2012, I was asked to contribute a piece to The Globe and Mail Report On Small Business page. I was then asked if I wanted to be a regular contributor writing about sales and selling. Talk about a "no brainer".

Since then, I have presented original pieces not found elsewhere. Some are on strategy, other talk tactics, some myth busting, and other observations from the front line of the revenue wars.

This compilation is a sample of some of my favourites, some that caused reaction, pro and much con, and some are just good fun.

I invite to read, consider, and put some of the suggestions into practice. Then let me know how it went.

Feel free to call me if something resonates, cause you to reconsider things, or if you want to talk about how you or your team sell.

If nothing else, please visit The Globe and Mail's Report On Small Business page (http://www.theglobeandmail.com/report-on-business/small-business/). You'll find my pieces every fourth Tuesday, and other great content from some insightful folks every day.

Thank you,
Tibor Shanto
tibor.shanto@sellbetter.ca

Are traditional sales methods dead?

Published November 06 2012 The Globe and Mail

There are a lot of questions about how small and medium-sized businesses can best make use of social media. Everyone is tweeting or talking about it, many salespeople are asking: "Should I abandon what I'm doing and embrace 'social selling,' or continue along the same path?"

The better question is: "How can I leverage both to achieve sales success?"

Sellers, like any other group, are a target for marketers who pitch them "things" to help them get better results. What makes salespeople good targets is their natural propensity to seek out "silver bullets" to deal with processes they don't like, and their deserved reputation as "early adopters." Just the right combination for the advent of "social selling."

We have seen the impact the Social Web and Web 2.0 have had on the way people interact, but it doesn't follow that social selling is driving the same changes in sales. Technology has always been an enabler, but from a business-to-business (B2B) sales standpoint, it has not changed the underlying nature or function of buying and selling, it has merely enhanced or enabled the way sales are executed.

Success is still very much about strategy and execution, driven by your market and your specific customers. You need to evaluate how you use social the same way you would with any other tools. Does it bring you closer to the buyer? Does it allow you to deliver your message and value in a way that helps buyers decide you are the provider to trust, partner with and have a relationship with? If so, then it needs to be part of the overall approach. If not, then as the saying goes: "A fool with a tool is still a fool."

Social selling impacts people pitching in the business-to-consumer (B2C) sales space differently than B2B, which is my focus. Despite the hype, the B2C social selling successes have not been realized in the B2B space – in the process, this distracts people and resources from things they could be doing to make social pay. The suggestion that traditional B2B sales strategies and tactics no longer work, and the notion that we need to abandon them for social selling or perish, is false, dangerous and a risky proposition for business owners.

What many people call social selling is, in reality, social marketing, which is why it's more effective in the mass B2C market than B2B. While it has a role in B2B, it is a role, not the entire sales process, as some might suggest. There are definitely times when social helps a sale, just as there are times when social has no positive impact, or even hurts your efforts.

For example, social tools can enhance awareness – generating leads or casting a more targeted net, the early steps of engaging with a potential buyer. Coincidentally, the part of a sale many sellers neither like nor are good at is prospecting. The perfect pitch for the wave of social-selling merchants is to offer a way to eliminate prospecting, but there are traditional steps you still need to take to initiate direct relationships.

The operative words in social media are "connect," "follow," "like," or "friend." In B2B selling, the focus is on direct contact: relationships, personal interaction, and occasionally intimate interaction between two people is crucial to success. Many social sellers advocate "being found" rather than taking an active approach to prospecting and initiating first contact with potential buyers. Social media may enhance direct interaction and relationships required in B2B sales, but it cannot replace them.

Social-selling pundits who create the illusion that a seller's role is to be "found" through the buyer's use of social media, give them all the excuse they need not to perform a key part of their job: prospecting. A simple question to start with is "how many of my customers are using social media to source the products or services I sell?" If few of your buyers are using social, very few will find you, no matter how well you do social.

Besides, being "found" works with buyers who decide to act on a need by going to the web. If they use search, they are less likely to be impacted by social selling. Even if they turn to their social sphere for peer input, traditional selling will play a major role in converting a connection to a direct interaction. By the time that buyer is on the web it's too late, you are competing with the pack. Use social media to identify, target and leverage trends, then execute a direct sale, and you will be there long before the social crowd.

A sound strategy to segmenting and targeting your market, then executing your plan with a combination of traditional marketing and social marketing, will take you further and faster than going strictly social. As with most trends, it's not a question of one versus the other, but how to leverage the best of both.

Stop trying to sell 'solutions' to potential customers

Published August 31, 2015 The Globe and Mail

There is a lot of talk about how sales has changed. When you get past the headlines, you find that the tools have changed, but how they are applied has not changed as much.

Having worked with many different types of sellers over the past 20-plus years, I am witness to the fact that one consistent focus for salespeople and organizations has been selling "solutions." Ask a group of salespeople "What do you sell?" and a good number will respond: "A solution." If that is you or your team, you are missing out on opportunities, limiting your potential, and working harder than you have to.

While solution selling may have been the way to go in the 1990s, it has lost its effectiveness because of advances in resources available to sellers and buyers. These have changed the landscape in a way that limits the impact of "solution selling."

First let's look at the concept of solutions. By definition, it is something that "solves" a problem.

When buyers had a problem, sales people could offer up a "solution." But today many of those buyers can source solutions on their own, leaving salespeople with less value, while chasing a smaller pie of potential buyers.

Add to that the fact that only a small part of the market has – or more accurately, recognizes or will admit to having – a problem, pain or need. Different sources place the proportion of the market actively looking for a product or service at between 3 per cent and 10 per cent. This is the portion of the market that has a problem, a need or a pain, something that needs solving or a solution.

These are the buyers you have heard about, the ones some two-thirds of the way through their buying journey before they reach out to a seller. This is directly a product of the available resources and access to information, but not necessarily knowledge. Buyers figure out what they want, and go shopping, playing a game of "price matching" or business-to-business (B2B) "showrooming," as though they were buying shoes. And sadly, most B2B vendors and sellers are happy to play.

There is a further 20 per cent or so, who are premarket, or people passively looking. They know they will have to make a purchase decision in the future, 12 to 24 months out, giving them lots of time to decide. These are good buyers to engage with. The long time frame and lack of attention from "solution sellers" gives you an opportunity to become their "go-to guy or gal" when they are in full active mode.

This leaves some 70 per cent of the market, the segment commonly labelled status quo, normally perceived as happy, satisfied and closed to change. Or put another way, no perceived problems, no pain, no need, and just because you see something (like a chance to retire quota), they don't. And without that, there is no need for a solution.

But there is one thing that all three groups, in fact, all businesses and business people have in common: They all have objectives.

Changing your focus to objectives from solutions has a number of immediate and continuing benefits. It will take time to change the focus from pain to gain. Start by reviewing your wins, losses and those opportunities that end in no decision, to understand which objectives are best to leverage.

Objectives are forward-looking, planned and ongoing, making them a much better common ground for growth than pain.

It will take time to reorient your sales organization to sell to this new audience, but the payoffs are worth it. And let's not forget, you can still sell to people with pain or need, but it will be in addition to, not instead of, a larger market segment.

Why customer satisfaction is overrated

Published May 12, 2015 The Globe and Mail

Soon enough Mick Jagger will be strutting his stuff across the stage, telling all who listen how he can't get no satisfaction.

Satisfaction is a key goal for many organizations. For example, salespeople search for customers who are dissatisfied with their current providers. In the process, they mistakenly ignore or overlook the large group of happy and "satisfied' potential buyers commonly referred to as "status quo. Customer support people send out surveys after every call to ensure the customer was "satisfied."

The problem with these tactics, however, is that satisfaction is a poor indicator for future revenue growth from a client and even retention.

For years pundits and sales managers encouraged their teams to focus on pain, need and the people who require their "solution," and by default, discouraged them from spending too much time chasing the status quo.

"They are happy and satisfied; they aren't open to change." This kind of thinking has led a number of salespeople to concentrate on a narrow and highly competitive part of the market. The 10 per cent or so who are actively looking and comparing you to your competitors and leveraging that for concessions (read discount). About another 20 per cent are those who are passively looking. They may have a machine that will be end of life in 18 months or so, they know they need to buy but feel they have time. It's a good group to pursue, but they're usually not enough to deliver quota. The remaining 70 per cent are the overlooked status quo, ignored because they are seemingly "satisfied."

But when you look at the stats, a different picture emerges. According to 'Customer Loyalty Guaranteed' Bell & Patterson, 75 per cent of customers who leave or switch vendors for a competitor, say they were 'satisfied or completely satisfied' with the vendor they left, at the time they switched. It's not the scenario you'd expect if you followed conventional wisdom. The question remains: why did this large group of satisfied customers jump ship? The answer is someone was able to find a motivator greater than fear, pain, needs, or satisfaction -- namely objectives.

While only a small segment of any given market may experience 'pain' or have a clearly defined need, everyone has objectives. Change the focus, change the narrative, and you change the outcome.

Pains and needs are short term. Once the client finds their 'Aspirin' they move on. Objectives, on the other hand, are forward-looking, uplifting and generally lead to more. Align your approach with their objectives, and the 70 per cent that is 'satisfied' will find a reason to move, to leave, mostly because they see a means of achieving their objectives. While they may be satisfied, and even like their current provider, they have been shown the greener grass on the other side of achieving their objectives. The effort in finding that out is not that much greater than finding their 'pain points,' but the payoff is bigger and longer lasting.

The contributing factor is how organizations view their clients. Once a company's first close takes place, it also shifts to 'satisfaction mode.' While this is fine for a while, remember that customers' objectives evolve and we need to evolve with them. A seller who understand her buyer's objectives, who engages and leads them to explore alternative views will easily connect with those motivated by pain and objectives.

The assumption that 'satisfied' customers will stay is problematic. You can have all the surveys you want saying that they are satisfied, if they see an opportunity to progress, to achieve a stated goal, they will reach for that every day and all day.

Rather than focusing on satisfaction, focus on aligning you entire customer-facing organization to focus on objectives. When you do, you'll be ready to welcome your competitors' satisfied customers.

Ten critical questions to ask during sales pipeline reviews

Published April 14, 2015 5:00AM EDT

As we head in to the second quarter, it's important that you have a solid pipeline, one that can be monetized over the next few months. Given the approaching summer season, this quarter – more so than any other – will determine how the rest of the year goes.

Now's the time to look into you funnel, take out the trash and replace it with real, closable opportunities.

Now's the time to look into you funnel, take out the trash and replace it with real, closable opportunities.

The following 10 questions will allow you to separate the good from the filler and go into this key quarter with a winning pipeline. If you're a sales representative, you should make a habit of asking these questions about every active opportunity in your funnel, each and every week. As a manager, make a habit of asking these questions about current active opportunities at every weekly meeting with the team. The great thing is that the answers come straight from interactions with prospects. If you're having those regularly, they will help keep you focused on the best opportunities.

1. **When's your next meeting?** If you don't know, you don't have a real prospect. Don't pretend that the opportunity is forecastable or that what you have is anything more than a questionable lead.

2. **When did you first engage?** Conversations are usually leads, not prospects - many people confuse the two. Conversations need to be nurtured and evolved to where they can be converted to prospects. Until that time they should not be in your pipeline.

3. **When was the last time you met?** If it's been longer than half of your average cycle, it's a lead. If they're not engaged and actively moving through the process with you, take them out and look for a replacement.

4. **How's the prospect dealing with or managing the area where you will add value?** If they're not choosing to deal with it now, what makes you think things will change? If they're managing now or if they managing fine without, why would they switch? If you can't answer these questions, you have a choice: go back to prospect and find out, or take them out of the funnel and find a real prospect or two to replace them.

5. **Why are they not using your product now?** This is an extension to the above question, but if you don't know this, you're operating in the dark.

6. **If this deal will close as you see it closing, what is the very next thing that has to happen?** If you can't answer this, go to jail and do not collect $200. As a sales professional this is fundamental: plan, execute, review.

7. **When and how will you make that happen?** This one's self-explanatory. Make it happen or make it go away.

8. **What does your prospect think is going to happen next?** If you don't know this, then you're working in the dark, and at risk of losing the deal or having to it go longer than it need be. What happens if you go in to close, and they think they're still defining requirements?

9. **Who or what are you up against?** How many times have you worked an opportunity only to be told that they had decided on an alternative you were not aware of. In these days of showrooming, how likely is it that you are alone, and if you are why? If you are not, you need to know who and why them.

10. **How badly does the prospect want the deal to happen?** While there may be no better way to gauge this than to ask, there are ways to test their resolve. If you haven't asked, what have you done to test things?

Your sales process is your last competitive advantage

Published March 17, 2015 The Globe and Mail

Most organizations understand the importance of their sales teams to drive revenue, but most undervalue how their sales processes can be a competitive advantage.

With due deference to product development, there's no escaping that most leading products have more things in common than not.

From a user perspective, line up the three leaders in any category and it's likely you'll find 80 per cent overlap in features and capabilities. So for all the talk of benefits, sizzle and zap, there's little to differentiate your product from others.

Because of this, why don't companies emphasize their sales process much more than they do? Many are happy to display their International Organization for Standardization (ISO) certifications. These are viewed as a useful means of adding credibility and "proof" that their products meet customer expectations.

Professionals within those same companies proudly display strings of the alphabet confirming their capabilities. In sales, the biggest accomplishment highlighted on a business card is President's Club. Along with your certifications, why not show off your company's training around sales process and ability to drive value for their clients?

The way your salespeople engage potential buyers and then take them though the buy/sell journey is often the only critical difference between winning and losing.

Yet most of the collateral is focused on product.

Some have always understood this and some may be old enough to remember the expression made famous in the 1980s "no one ever got fired for buying IBM." While many in the know tell me Digital Equipment Corp. (DEC) had an equal if not superior product, IBM outsold them, winning by focusing on the short game – where it really counts.

To make this work, you first need to map out the buy/sell journey. Many teams do have a sales process, but it isn't always adhered to, making it difficult to leverage as a differentiator. A sales-flow or process aligns the seller with the buyer, and recognizes the clients' role beyond writing a check.

A sales process where the central feature is the buyer's objectives and the seller's subject matter expertise can lead to a much more productive discussion, leading to shorter cycles, more wins, and greater client loyalty, because their objectives would be the continuing focus.
This process, tied to standards around execution can give a seller the similar advantages to ISO. Imagine putting that on your brochures and having sales people leverage it during calls.

Another factor that will help you make this work is an ongoing investment in your front-line managers. While many organizations talk about being committed to coaching, few do an adequate job of helping their sales managers become better coaches. This is even more pronounced when managers are former sales stars promoted into the role without much help in transitioning. Left to their own devices, they will attempt to clone themselves. If they were developed as coaches, they wouldn't only enhance the client experience, but drive more sales. Studies have shown that regular and consistent coaching, some would suggest daily, leads to a 17 per cent increase in revenue by reps coached.

Although the step listed above are not easy to take, they're nowhere near as difficult as getting buy-in from senior corporate and sales leaders. And while I appreciate the pressures to hit monthly and quarterly sales, it should not be at the expense of long term success.

It's really a question of continuing down the path you are on, hoping buyers see some merit in your product or marketing's messaging; or leveraging the only real differentiator and advantage, your sales team and its process.

In sales circles, information is currency but knowledge is power

Published November 18, 2014 The Globe and Mail

There's been a lot of talk recently about the diminishing need for salespeople. Part of the argument stems from the fact that buyers, apparently, are better informed than ever. Pundits tell us that things have turned upside down; it's now the era of 'seller beware,' because buyers have greater access to more information and data. But does access to more information actually mean the customer is better informed? Does it really position buyers to make the right decisions?

When looking for the right decision, the old adage 'less is more' may serve decision makers well. John Payne, professor at the Duke Institute for Brain Sciences[1], argues that information overload can actually hamper good decision making:

He maintains the most common results of information overload and its impact on decisions include:

Decision avoidance or procrastination. This isn't something sales people want.

Selection of the default. The customer stays with what they know, who they are working with now, classic status quo.

Reverting to simple heuristics. This may lead to a customer choosing the lowest cost provider rather than best fit.

It's true that buyers have access to more information, but there's nothing that supports the idea that they are making better decisions as a result. Further, there is no support for the notion that to make the right decision they need sales people any less. The opposite argument is likely more accurate.

---

[1] http://www.dibs.duke.edu/

First, access does not equal use especially when access is in the form of a fire hose aimed at your face. At some point people shut down, and that point is tied directly to volume – not quality – of information. Filtering, combined with setting objectives in advance is one way decision makers cope. For a seller the opportunity is to influence the filters, not pile on more content for the consumer to sift through. If a salesperson can influence the filters, much like some salespeople influence RFPs they have a direct impact on the decision. This involves focusing on buyers' objectives, and helping them align the information to specifics which drive the outcomes. The objective seller not only filters but synthesizes information into actionable knowledge that leads to desired outcomes. Working back from objectives helps salespeople deliver the right information unencumbered by noise.

As technology advances, the information fire hose will continue to spray at a higher speed than ever before. In fact, as Google executive chairman Eric Schmidt[2] pointed out[3], every two days now we create as much information as we did from the dawn of civilization up until 2003. And that statement was made in August 2010. Some believe there is so much information and data being produced, there may be a shortage of storage capacity.

Pity the decision maker. Another challenge is that information comes in many forms, from fantasy to expert or independently validated facts and all points in between. Today's social platforms allow people with ill-informed opinions to appear as information sources. Decision makers can often separate the good from the questionable, but not always. With excess information available, knowledge becomes more valuable and hyper commoditized. In turn, this leaves real decision makers not only wanting, but seeking knowledgeable sources in making the right decision.

Superior salespeople strive to be subject matter experts and conduits for best practices. This allows them to talk about outcomes and the process of achieving them, which often has less to do with product or service, and more with understanding the buyer's end goal and competitive landscape. As the saying goes, if my job is to drill the perfect quarter-inch hole, you should be selling me the hole, not the drill. All the information about the drill will do nothing for me. But knowledge about the hole will

[2] http://www.crunchbase.com/person/eric-schmidt
[3] http://techcrunch.com/2010/08/04/schmidt-data/

drive conversation and decisions. Being that conduit is different than being an information curator or content marketer. When decision makers are looking to improve their bottom line, they want someone who can bottom line it for them, not dump it on them.

Technology is the great sales equalizer

Published January 22 2013 The Globe and Mail

If you grew up with Disney you know it's a small world, made even smaller by technology, the Internet, and social media. The impact on different sectors and companies has varied, in both good and bad ways.

In sales, social media has proven to be the great equalizer.

Large companies traditionally had a great advantage in the client-acquisition process, from marketing – including
lead generation – to engaging potential buyers. They could not only leverage their budgets, they also had multi-regional resources to establish their brands and to raise awareness, giving them the ability to more readily convert prospects to clients.

But social, both the tools and trends, have levelled the playing field, allowing small businesses to compete and even out-do larger players when it comes to winning the hearts, minds and budgets of buyers.

It used to be that mounting a sustained and successful campaign to market, sell to, and maintain customers required more money, resources and time than many small and medium-sized businesses (SMBs) could afford. While the Internet and advances in logistics allowed SMBs to expand their reach, much of that demand found them – it wasn't the result of specific steps they took to create and attract the business.

Social media changed the game, including how businesses view their client-acquisition processes and execution. Companies, no matter how small, can develop and implement an effective campaign by leveraging social media, targeting very specific buyers of their product, with a budget not much greater than that required for traditional vehicles.

No longer limited by barriers between sales and marketing, which existed more because of the tools available than due to a specific need, companies can now take a truly holistic view. Evidence can be seen in the rise of chief revenue officers or directors of revenue, who now have the responsibility and the ability to drive business throughout the client life cycle. They can use social to better nurture and score leads before moving opportunities down the assembly line to sales.

Social then can provide better air cover for the sales "ground troops," while at the same time allowing them to establish their brand alongside that of the company. Finally, social can play a key role in enhancing the retention and penetration stage. All of this can be done just as effectively and, one could argue, with more creativity than it can be by larger companies with proportionally greater marketing and sales resources deployed in more traditional (or Web 1.0) ways.

People are increasingly interacting with social media and consuming information on mobile devices. Tools designed for those users provide better targeting, often with lower costs. General applications such as Hootsuite[1] and Tweedadder[2] allow you to identify potential buyers, to find out what your customers are saying, and to prospect specific individuals or groups.

Another trend social allows sellers to leverage is geo-sensing. Local sellers can compete based on their proximity to buyers without necessarily sacrificing the broader "global" market. "Increasingly, geo-sensing search and geo-location are becoming critical in search and other kinds of online (primarily mobile) online interactions," says Dr. James Norrie, associate professor at Ryerson University in Toronto. "In our

---

[1] http://hootsuite.com/
[2] http://tweedadder.com/

practice, we have corrupted the original term 'glocal' to indicate global, local search. That is, accessible and visible globally, but the emphasis on locally originated and serviced searches and hits."

As people continue to converge their consumption of traditional media, social media and search into one seamless environment, using tools such as Flipboard[3], smaller local sellers can heighten their visibility to local buyers with geo, without sacrificing global prospects who seek them out based on subject tags used to pinpoint their messages.

It won't be long before business-to-business sellers have tools that give them the ability to interact with prospects in the same way individual consumer-oriented sellers use apps such as Foursquare[4]. How long before big and small businesses take advantage of Facebook's recently announced "graph search" to go beyond connecting and mapping relationships to connecting and mapping people to products.

With social tools, the world is flat again, and SMB sellers are on equal footing with bigger and broader competitors.

---

[3] http://flipboard.com/
[4] http://foursquare.com/

Training Won't Fix Your Systemic Problems

Published August 04, 2015 The Globe and Mail

One of the most important roles sales leaders have is to ensure their sales organization is performing to its maximum capability. They must to ensure systems, processes, and people, are aligned and optimized. When there is misalignment, and performance (results) falls short, they have to identify the issue, act decisively to resolve it and move forward. Part of that accountability is acting honestly and boldly to address the specific issue.

But there are many leaders who deliberately ignore the real problem, in favour of the easy way out.

For example, when the issue is systemic, they turn to skills training, because it is the easier option. But "doing something" instead of the "right thing" is no more than covering up the problem with a thin veneer or fresh coat of paint, often leading to setbacks instead. Like when companies rolled out CRM's, only automate and accelerate existing problems.

Often this type of training leads to nothing more than becoming a stick with which to beat the sales team for not achieving something that is almost impossible to achieve due to systemic problems. Failing to recognize this and genuinely dealing the real systemic issues is like putting a Band-Aid on a broken leg, you won't see the bruising, but you won't walk on it either. Systemic changes are hard, training offers an easy option out.

One example of this is a lack of consequences for non-performance, something hardly tolerated in other areas of the organization. A downside of the popular 80/20 rule, is the systemization of mediocrity. By accepting the standard as many have, that 80% of your revenue comes from 20% of your reps (not always true, but too many pay it lip service), you are systemizing failure. The 80% are not just given permission to fail, but are almost encouraged, if not challenged to. Seems to me if you got rid of the bottom half of the 80%, you'd not only save on labour costs, but set a fire under the other half, and drive success.

There is a lot of lip service paid to Jack Welch's managing out of the bottom 10%. Yet when it comes to pruning sales teams, nothing! The monies saved in commission to the bottom half, can be used to truly reward performers, and to reduce your cost of sales at the same time. Allowing people to linger and not perform is a systemic issue, and throwing more training at people who should be waiting tables instead of selling will not change that.

This problem presents itself at all levels of the organization, and at times driven from the top. I've seen companies keep the most useless sales people for gender balance, for fear of having a vacant territory, because they liked someone who had been with the company for some time, or a host of other lame reasons. Other times it is at the VP level, classic Status Quo, they fear change more than the cancer they are living with. Whether they let their ranks get away with it, or they fail to see things for what they are, they breeding mediocrity, the mold that plagues many sales organizations. It always ends with the same refrain, "Well what can I do, you can't fire them all". Yes you can, maybe it should start with the top.

A related systemic challenge is the ADHD mentality running up and down sales organizations. Most want to pretend that training is an event, add water and presto, sales are up. Fixing a systemic problem not only takes guts and vision, but time. There is no escaping that at times the only long-term solution is to break it and start again. Raze and build, works for civilizations, urban planning, and sales organizations. But in an age of instant gratification, and obsession with quarterly monthly and weekly results, few have the vision and kahunas to drive real change and approach a systematic path to improvement. It is a lot easier and flashier to throw a coat of training paint on it, and kick things down the road.

Given that most sales leaders will explain to you why the local sports franchise may take seasons to rebuild, there seems to be little resolve to allow a similar view to their own success, that of their team and company, to undergo a similar transformation and return to long term consistent success.

How to reduce turnover in your sales force

Published July 08, 2015 The Globe and Mail

Turnover in the sales ranks is a challenge for many companies, and some industries regularly experience turnover as high as 40 per cent a year. This attrition is due to a number of factors, including fit, abilities, and the front-line managers' ability to lead. But the most overlooked factor in turnover and ensuring success is the on-boarding process. The means by which you assimilate the new recruit into your culture can be the singular difference between success and failure with a new sales rep – and the return on your recruitment dollars.

The main problem in sales is that the whole process of finding and integrating on sales talent is disjointed. Sourcing, vetting, introducing reps to the team and ensuring rapid and continuous success should be one seamless process, but it's often a series of siloed activities. What should be a coordinated roadmap and execution often ends up being a series of hand-offs.

The human resources department will work with the hiring manager to develop a job description, then add some of their own spice to the mix. They will often work with a recruiting firm to source candidates, with the recruiter having no contact with the candidates' future manager and they may or may not participate in the interview process. When the recruit is complete, they hand off the candidate, offering a guarantee for a period of time in case the candidate does not work out.

HR will orient the recruit to the company, helping with policies, benefits, security passes, computer and other tools. This may include a "quick start" or "jump start" training, a week of product training, order entry, basic sales training, and an introduction to the companies' sales process. That is if they have a sales process, which is not always a given.

I remember asking a VP of sales from a sizable company about their sales process, he told me "yes we have one, salesforce.com." It's a great CRM, not a sales process. Not having a process brings a number of impediments to sales success, including improper on-boarding of reps.

When HR completes their tasks, they offload the candidate to sales, usually the front line manager. Most managers do not have a plan for new reps. Some will take some specific steps, for example, spending a bit more time with them or going on a few calls, but generally there's no overall plan. They often overestimate the employee's level of preparation.

A better plan is to have all three parties–HR, the recruiter, and the front line manager and a trainer–work together in developing and rolling out a seamless on-boarding plan, one that starts well before the offer, and lasts much longer than many current on-boarding initiatives. There should be clear objectives and milestones along the way, the timeline should be at least as long as three times the length of your sales cycle. This allows for onboarding to be phased and aligned with success elements as needed based on your sale and process, rather than an info and policy dump when they start, when it has no meaning or context.

The model I like is creating a partnership with the recruiter, HR, the manager, and myself, the trainer. As the short list is developed, we examine the strengths and weaknesses of the candidates, and begin to formulate the sales training plan with the manager before offers are made. When the rep is hired, there is no handoff. The recruiter, manager and I are already engaged. This all happens as long as a month prior to the hire's start date. These plans can be as long as year, usually much longer than the guarantee, which usually does not get triggered.

Sure, it's more work upfront, but the payoff is big: You'll benefit from reduced recruiting costs, better retention rates, improved customer satisfaction, and greater revenue down the road.

A few small sales tweaks can have big revenue impact

Published March 19 2013 The Globe and Mail

There is a school of thought in business-to-business (B2B) selling that a sales organization, and its individual reps, should know by the end of the first quarter whether they'll make their quota by year end. For the most part, this is a good line of thought to subscribe to.

As we approach the end of this year's first quarter, it's a good time to step back and review your progress, the state of your current sales, and your pipeline.

This is the time to make adjustments to your sales strategy and execution. If you're on track or ahead, you can explore how to accelerate your success, how to leverage the things that are going well, and how to benefit from the momentum you created in the first quarter. On the other hand, if you are behind in your goal, it's still early enough to make adjustments, to get back on track and to deliver the kind of year you want. Based on the nature of your business and its revenue patterns, you will require different types of corrections.

Avoid wholesale knee-jerk or reactionary changes, not because drastic is bad but because it consumes key resources – not the least of which is time, your only non-renewable resource. Big projects have little chance of showing returns before year end, which defeats the exercise. Not to sound conservative, but it's more practical to think about executing specific incremental and tactical things that can have immediate impact.

One reality of wholesale change is that it often replaces what exists rather than building on what is working and then adjusting for other elements. Unless you have drastically missed your sales targets for years, you probably have a good starting plan that would benefit from fine tuning or reinforcement, rather than a complete discard.

One of the most effective things you can do is step back and take a dispassionate look at your sales pipeline and its components. People are very subjective about their pipeline, and the emotional attachment clouds their judgment, and it limits their activities at critical stages of the sales cycle. There are a number of basic pipeline metrics you should be tracking and analyzing, regardless of whether you are at your goal, above it or below. These include conversion rates and coverage levels.

While this is in no way exhaustive, here are a few to consider:

- Lead to engagement
- Engagement to proposal
- Proposal to close

A small and very achievable uptick in any or all of these conversion rates can have a dramatic multiplier effect on the results. If you improved just two of these activities by only 10 per cent each, the overall impact on revenues is some 17 per cent, as the chart shows.

	Current state	Incremental improvement	Uptick in	Impact	
Engagements	12		0	12	
(Engage to proposal)	*33%*	*10%*	*36.7%*		
Proposals	4			**4.4**	
(Proposals to close)	*50%*	*10%*	*55%*		
Deals closed	2			**2.42**	
Average deal in $$	$20,000			$20,000	
Total monthly revenues	**$40,000**			**$48,400**	**17%**

If you were to improve all three by the same 10 per cent, you would see a 25 per cent improvement in revenues. To stretch a bit further, if you held your price and increased your price by 5%, the overall gain would be 32%, but let's not push it.

The beauty of this is that you can pick two of these areas to be more effective in – and remember, you or your team are already doing them, so it's an adjustment not an overhaul. If, on the other hand, you don't know these simple metrics, the first thing you might need to do is start tracking them. You don't need a big customer relationship management (CRM) app, you can use tools you already have, such as a pen and paper. It is the tracking and doing that are important.

Pipeline coverage is another lever available for incremental improvement. I'm not talking about piling on prospects, but having the right level. Too few real prospects forces you to spend too much time and energy trying to convert everything, worthwhile or not, because it is the only thing you have.

You cut corners, or discount, because if you don't you'll miss out. Too many prospects crowd out the best opportunities, again requiring extra effort and time just to sort through. Knowing the above conversion rates allows you to know what the optimal coverage level should be, and gives you time to target more of the right prospects. The level is specific to each rep or organization, allowing them to make the right adjustments for the right multiplier effect.

So before spending time, money and resources, and stressing out about the changes needed to get back on track to achieve your goals by year end, pick one or two doable things, make the adjustment, and move forward.

Your sales team needs more practice

Published September 28, 2015 The Globe and Mail

I am often asked by small- and medium-sized business owners and managers in larger companies what steps they can take to help their sales people perform more effectively. The answer rests with them. But when told what needs to be done, many fail to step up, primarily because it requires a greater effort than they are willing to make.

As with almost any other professional endeavour, a critical element of success is practice and coaching: Two things you don't see enough in sales, and which owners and managers could do a better job of initiating and enforcing.

Let's first look at coaching. Success in any organization comes down to leadership, and in sales especially, the front-line leadership, be that the business owner or front-line manager. Effective sales managers need to create and maintain a balance between two personas. The first is as the "manager," who sets the rules and expectations for the sales team. While this may seem obvious, I continuously run into scenarios where the expectations are not set or clear, allowing sales people to do it "their way," which no doubt explains why a North American survey found that less than 60 per cent of B2B reps made their quota in 2014.

With expectations set – be they around activity, meeting objectives, use of tools, what have you – the next persona that needs to be adopted is that of the "coach," helping the team and individual members deliver on those expectations. In professional sports this is often carried out by specialist individuals, such as the pitching coach or the batting coach in baseball, for example. Most sales teams, especially non-enterprise or small businesses cannot afford these to have people in these individual roles, and so it is down to the manager or owner.

This is the part that is usually lacking; it requires more effort than just setting goals and firing up the old rah-rah – it requires planning and consistent effort in application. It's not just a matter of designing the playbook, but creating the drills, and doing them over and over till the team and individuals get it right. In larger companies many of the managers I speak with have no annual coaching plan, and smaller companies don't see the need. "I hired professionals; they are beyond that," is what I often hear.

Getting it right requires practice by sales people, yet practising is not something many do, or concede they need to do. Again, just as they would expect from their favourite team, the hard work is between games, not just when they are on the pitch. It seems newsworthy when a player misses practice or a team is given a day off, but ask sales people if they practised or rehearsed for that sales call and see what you get for an answer.

Experts tell us that it takes an enormous amount of preparation and practice to deliver an effective presentation. Some say an hour for every 10 minutes; others say you should practice each presentation 15 times or more. And this is for a one-way presentation, not an interactive dialogue where the buyer will always throw unexpected questions at you. People who make it look easy, such as Steve Jobs and Charlie Parker, practised constantly to be as good as they were.

Many sellers and managers will tell you that they just don't have the time to invest in that much practice, despite study after study that show the impact of coaching in increasing revenues. The most effective sales companies provide 15 to 20 per cent more coaching, with the key being not how elaborate a coaching discipline is, but how consistent. Not only can coaching lead to better revenue attainment, but the time invested can be recouped in shorter sales cycles.

There is no denying that practice take time and effort, but there is also no denying that practice makes profits.

Why great salespeople are more blue-collar than white-collar

Published April 16 2013 The Globe and Mail

I've seen a lot of people gravitate toward sales, seeing it as a rewarding white-collar career – with a little skill, a lot of personality, and a bit of luck or "timing" they think they can succeed. We all know individuals who are described as natural-born salespeople.

But career salespeople – more specifically, consistently successful salespeople – are a group of professionals who realize that success requires hard work, constant improvement, and execution.

The "naturals" will always point out that they have "15 years of experience." Unfortunately, more often than not, it is the same year 15 times over, rather than 15 years of improvements, consistent results and contributions to their businesses. Business-to-business selling is as much blue-collar work as building something from the ground up, including the planning, the heavy lifting and the finishing.

A blue-collar seller is more likely to focus on and speak about the process, the execution and the outcome, while the white-collar seller tends to focus on the relationship, often putting it ahead of deals and revenue. The latter tend to prefer speaking about the finesse or art of what they are (or are not) doing, rather than whatever it takes to get the sale. You need to have and maintain good relationships with your customers, but the reality is that those relationships usually evolve over time after initial sales, rather than being formed first and then realizing sales over time.

Salespeople have never been paid commission for forming relationships with potential buyers. They develop solid connections with people who initially see them as vendors who can demonstrate how their offers add value to buyers' objectives. Relationships normally flourish as a result of satisfaction with the early purchases.

It's an age-old question: Is sales an art or a science? The white-collar seller will default to the former, but the risk is that art is subjective – it allows sellers to avoid the accountability that comes with process and metrics.

Sales is a science executed artfully. Blue-collar sellers are like good musicians – they know they need to learn the eight notes, chord progressions, and so on, that will give them the grounding to improvise the way Charlie Parker did. While the improvisation is the art, Mr. Parker practiced for hours a day for years. When was the last time your sales reps practiced for three or four hours a day?

The blue-collar sellers understand that while finesse, diplomacy and sensitivity are important, they also know sales is a contact sport. It's less like figure skating – where judges hold up scores for artistic merit – and more like football, where you work a plan to move the ball down field and you are measured by the outcome. While you may get credit for the finesse of your playmaking, what counts is getting the ball over the goal line and the score at the end of the game.

Unlike many white-collar sellers who will tell you "no, I couldn't do that," the blue-collar seller will do what it ethically takes to score, even if it's not pretty or it gets mud on their boots.

While I see these two approaches unfold every day, the case for the blue-collar method is much more compelling and sustainable in both up and down economies. The position was recently reinforced in an interview on CNBC, when Sir Martin Sorrell, CEO of WPP Group, described the state of his business, the challenges, the opportunities and the levers available to his employees to deliver results.

While they got where they wanted to go, as he puts it, they "got there ugly."

Salespeople who provoke 'in the right way' will outperform

Published July 09 2013 The Globe and Mail

When you look back and think about who has had the most profound influence and impact on your life, you probably remember the people who challenged you most, who created discomfort, who pushed you, and who felt like they were a huge pain while taking you to new heights. They have likely left a lasting positive impact on how you turned out.

Maybe there was a teacher who kept on you until you got the answer "the right way," or a hockey coach who moved you from third stringer to starter by being "in your face." If you've done military service, there might have been a drill sergeant who wouldn't accept "okay." These people believed you could do more, and they made it their mission to make you great by not letting up, by doubling down and challenging you to stretch, which validated their efforts and their belief in you.

Now think about people in your private or professional life – friends, colleagues, "good relationships," many forgotten – who rarely come to mind when you think about impact or influence.

What makes these two groups different?

The former focused on your desires, objectives and abilities. They were willing to do whatever it took to get you there – they didn't get hung up on whether they were making you uncomfortable by confronting your viewpoints, convictions and limits. They pushed you to expand your horizons – at times vigorously and in a hands-on way – taking you closer to your goals. They respected your vision and enhanced your abilities.

Members of the other group were probably more concerned about building and maintaining relationships than they were about the outcomes. Not wanting to rock the boat, they cared more about appearances and your comfort than your objectives – keeping things easy in the process.

Outstanding results don't, as a rule, come easy. Breakthroughs take work. Rationalizing results is very different than doing what it takes to remove obstacles to action and success. Many in the latter group place a higher value on how you feel than what you can achieve, which respects your space but not your real abilities or real objectives.

Let's take these two scenarios and apply them to a sales situation, where the subject is the buyer, and the person having – or not having – impact is the seller.

Which of the two groups do you think is more successful over the long term, drives more revenue and profit, and makes more money? Just as important: Which one is in greater demand?

Salespeople with the ability to provoke in the right way for the right reasons and who often vigorously challenge buyers will always outperform passive relationship sellers or sales "facilitators." This is especially true as buyers continue to bypass relationships and purchase from other parties, a trend that has accelerated in the past few years. One big reason for this is that there are sellers approaching customers you have "relationships" with who are pushing them beyond their current horizons and comforts – in other words, beyond you – leading to new areas of discussion, valuation and sales. These sellers are provoking buyers in a number of ways, but they're all tied to buyer objectives. Buyers will tolerate being pushed if they understand the intent is helping them achieve.

Just as you will tolerate a line of questioning from a lawyer or doctor – understanding their intent and the beneficial outcome – buyers will too, if you can demonstrate that your intent is to help them.

Provocative sellers understand and leverage people's averseness to risk. The fact that 70 per cent of the population is risk averse has been a barrier to change, both in buying habits and the propensity to act, especially given the risk of the unknown. "Better the devil you know" has been a great friend to the relationship seller, but not always to their buyers.

Raising the risk profile of a buyer, and making the "do nothing" option more risky than something new and different, takes a direct and, at times, aggressive approach. Not by browbeating, or by being rude or belligerent, but by asking the hard questions around a buyer's real objectives and obstacles, and the risk of not achieving them.

Given the right intent, executed professionally, there is no reason your buyer should not feel the same elation you did when your teacher pushed you to get that A on the final exam.

Lesson from Starbucks: Quality and consistency are worth paying for

Published August 06 2013 The Globe and Mail

Price is always a touchy issue for salespeople, even more so in today's environment. Not only because the economy has made everyone more price sensitive, but also because active buyers engage their own networks before they do sellers. Furthermore, buyers are more informed about your product and specifically your price.

Salespeople don't want to win or lose strictly on that singular factor, but often do. While some companies and salespeople have given into discounting, others resist, and work to maintain price integrity while not losing revenue or clients. This is the exact discussion I had with a sales manager last week at Starbucks[1]. She was lamenting the number of deals decided on price alone, regardless of quality differences.

Starbucks was an interesting place to have this discussion. People who know me will tell you that coffee is one of my few vices; four or five cups before 9 a.m. – easily a dozen by days end. I go to the coffee chain not because they are the best, but because I appreciate the quality, consistency and predictability of the experience. No matter if I am in Toronto, Las Vegas, London or Grand Rapids, the experience is consistent. Put this way: when it comes to the nectar of the gods, I don't want any surprises. I want the hit I am expecting and that's exactly what Starbucks gives me – from the surroundings, the atmosphere, the coffee, to the disciples of Landru[2] baristas. All satisfying my expectations, Starbucks provides a predictability I find worth paying a premium for.

---

[1] http://www.theglobeandmail.com/globe-investor/markets/stocks/chart/?q=SBUX-Q
[2] http://www.startrek.com/database_article/landru

The added bonus of my coffee addiction is the daily reminder that I don't have to be the lowest cost provider to consistently win business, even when there are alternatives that offer more than an incremental price advantage. Just as I think the difference is worthwhile, you too can find and sell to buyers willing to pay a premium for what you have, when you focus and sell them based on those specific elements.

In fact, you're probably doing this but aren't completely aware of it, and therefore not fully leveraging it. Rather than me proving this, you can do it for yourself. Ask your top 5 to ten clients the following: 'Why do you deal with me and my company?"

What you'll find in almost all cases price is not at the top of the list. In fact, it rarely appears in the top three. What will be on the list are some of the attributes listed below:

- Understanding and helping their Business
- Thought leadership Unique expertise/perspectives
- Ease of relationship, including problem resolution
- Challenge and educate
- Reliability
- Dependability
- Reacting to their needs
- Innovativeness – R&D
- Total product offering – Total cost of Ownership
- Technical education
- Frequency of sales calls
- Preparedness for sales calls

Knowing specifically which attributes resonate with your clients will help you develop talking points and talk tracks. In turn, this will lead to a similar quality discussion with potential buyers who value those elements, and are willing to pay full value or a premium. Others who don't care about those attributes are likely the buyers who won't pay, giving you the comfort to move on rather than engage in fruitless time consuming negotiations and frustrations. Those that don't fit will be there once you have exhausted all the opportunities with those who do fit, with likely shorter sales cycles and more rewarding ongoing relationships.

The exercise will also start you implementing a best practice used by most successful sales teams, deal reviews. Reviewing why deals turned out the way they did has a number of dividends. But unlike what some pundits will tell you, the key is to review all deal types, not just one type. Only reviewing your wins or loses is fraught with risk and can result in tunnel vision. Instead try looking at all three deal outcomes: wins, losses and 'no decisions.' It doesn't take much time but the resulting insights are invaluable.

Price is in the eyes of the beholder, it's up to you to target and engage with those who will see it in context. Time for a coffee.

Cold calling comes back from the dead

Published September 03 2013 The Globe and Mail

Zombies have made a comeback, though you could argue they never went away, from Night of the Living Dead[1] to World War Z[2] and points in between (who could forget Shaun of the Dead[3]?).

What do zombies have to do with sales? One reason I have a soft spot for the undead is that I'm still a firm believer in cold calling and its importance to any business – to – business prospecting and client acquisition regimen. But on a regular basis some pundit will proclaim as loud as possible: COLD CALLING IS DEAD.

Next thing you know, it comes back to life, minus the rotting flesh.

In the past I have challenged "no more cold calling" messiahs to debate the issue, only to have them turn down the opportunity. I suspect it's because many of these experts are pandering to the crowd and they are offering little more than the sales version of those late-night infomercial ab-firming machine peddlers.

What set me off this time was a piece on Forbes.com titled Cold Calling is Dead, Thanks to LinkedIn[1], which makes the same mistake as previous attacks, namely they are aiming at the wrong part of the beast. The author states: "LinkedIn is the single most powerful sales information tool on the planet. It makes it so you don't have to cold call … ever!"

Well, that's only half true. Successful cold calling consists of two dynamics. Yes, LinkedIn is great and it has dramatically improved the ability of sellers to be informed

---

[1] http://www.imdb.com/title/tt0063350/

[2] http://www.imdb.com/title/tt0816711/

[3] http://www.imdb.com/title/tt0365748/?ref_=fn_al_tt_1

[1] http://www.forbes.com/sites/kenrogue/2013/08/09/cold-calling-is-dead-thanks-to-linkedin/

and better prepared for engagement. If you're not using it, you are missing out. But what makes the cold call scary for many is not the information dynamic, it's the execution. It's that last nerve-wracking step where you have to interrupt someone, then transition to a conversation – a point the soothsayers always fail to address, but without it, just being informed will help little.

No matter how informed and ready you are, unless you are on someone's calendar, the moment you call you are an interruption and therefore prone to being rejected. This is true even when you are referred, unless the person referring you initially contacted the person you are calling. The real reason people want to avoid cold calling is the awkwardness and fear of rejection – just look at the comments on the Forbes piece.

With demands on people's time, no one can afford distractions. Faced with the choice of completing work or being interrupted, they will choose work and "reject" the caller. Managing the rejection makes good cold callers, and that's the case to a much larger degree than how informed they may be. Even if you – like all the salespeople using LinkedIn – say something truly compelling, you need to deal with that primal instinct and reaction.

Great salespeople always had good networks, good sources of information, and the ability to engage around an issue, but they also knew the first hurdle is the dynamic. Unless you master how to manage and navigate that initial moment, you're never more than halfway there.

The numbers

DiscoverOrg[1] recently surveyed 1,000 IT decision makers at Fortune ranked, small and medium-sized companies. It shows how outbound – today's euphemism for cold – sales calls and e-mails affect and "more importantly disrupt vendor selection."

"Seventy-five per cent of IT executives have set an appointment or attended an event as a direct result of outbound email and call techniques." Further, "nearly 600 said an outbound call or e-mail led to an IT vendor being evaluated."
An opportunity that only happened due to cold calling.

---

[1] http://discoverorg.com/its-all-about-outbound/

Last month I presented at a gathering of owners and principals of IT-related dealers, ranging from $3-million to $10-million in sales. I asked how many of them had LinkedIn profiles, and less than 10 did. There's a lot of money in that void.

The reality is that effective prospecting and buyer engagement should never come down to one approach versus the other. The greatest success comes from leveraging an integrated approach. The one versus another is usually promoted by those who don't understand one, so they sell the other.

Planning to whip your sales team into shape? Don't expect instant results

Published January 14 2014 The Globe and Mail

The New Year is a time for resolutions and commitments to new things, or just old commitments revisited. Despite best intentions, most will revert back to their old ways, if not completely, at good 90 per cent of the way.

Go to any gym the first ten days of the year, the regular patrons are all out of sorts because of all the new people crowding the floor, being a general nuisance, posing for the mirror, while blocking access to your favourite equipment. But we all know that it's just a question of days – at worst a couple of weeks – before these non-committed wannabees disappear, allowing us to enjoy our workouts once more.

Resolutions made by sales people and sales organization are no different and often suffer the same fate. At times, these resolutions are tied to the calendar, at an annual kick-off, or some significant event.

I remember one company I worked for tied the new-us-new-way-we-sell to the roll out of a CRM. Some of these sales-resolutions survive as a result of a strong and charismatic leader, but most fade. The cause is not so much negative, as it is a misunderstanding of change, and the monumental effort it take to introduced, but exponential effort required to perpetuate the change introduce. Couple that with the fact that often the change is much more ambitious than it needs to be; like swinging for the fences when a simple bunt will get the job done.

Real change requires major overhauls in habits, just as quitting smoking, for example, often requires giving up coffee or other indulgences. Weight loss takes more than just a diet: it involves a lifestyle change that is often more difficult than simply reducing or altering the amount of food being consumed.

To achieve the change we want, we must start by razing a host of interrelated current habits. This is difficult enough for most, not to mention the greater effort involved in sustaining any gains made. Many sellers use the challenges in the many related areas, as an easy reason to rationalize giving up on the thing we initially set out to change.

Change comes from the core, not the periphery. This is especially true for sales organizations. Many people spend their time tinkering with a few marginal elements, ignoring key core elements, setting themselves up for failure before they start. For example, they organizations demand that their front-line field representatives change their focus, but don't make changes in the order processing, fulfillment or other procedures that could help them succeed.

So what can organizations do to help their salespeople succeed? It could be as simple as updating the sales process to help the reps adjust how they sell, or explaining how Customer Relationship Management (CRM) or other applications can help or impact their selling or sales.

By far the biggest mistake sales organizations make is underestimating what truly is required to truly sustain change over time. They fail to realize – or, worst – accept that the kind of change they seek, and resolve to implement takes months or even years.

Making your changes stick involves a level of commitment many individuals and or organizations are not prepared or just plain lack the guts to make. I have lost many engagements when stakeholders were told that we will need many months, not a few weeks. The best results are realized by companies who mark initiatives in years.

Many, like the posers at the gym, expect instant results. They marvel at the slightest sign of change early in the process, call it success and fail to see it as the first step in a long journey. As the initiative inevitably fails, the organization retreats to their old ways, senior management reverts back to their old battle cries, confirming the end of another failed experiments.

The immediate effect and lingering damage of this recurring ritual is that front line reps lose faith, and not so much resist change, but learn to ignore it. Their modus operandi is to keep their heads down for a few weeks and their mantra becomes "this too shall pass."

My biggest customer was a hippie. Is yours a millennial?

Published April 08 2014 The Globe and Mail

In early March, NBC Nightly News ran a segment called: By the numbers: 'Who are the Millennials?' based on a report by Pew Research Center. What struck me most were the similarities to other generational groups, including the baby boomers and hippies. I also started thinking of the implications on business-to-business (B2B) selling and buying. As a 1957 Cynic – with my go-to song "Won't Get Fooled Again" – I witnessed hippies slowly (but surely) transform into all the things they railed against as they listened to "My Generation" during the summer of love.

The report highlighted some key differences, especially as they relates to technology and media consumption; hippies guarded their personal privacy, while millennials are happy to trade it for a round of Angry Birds. Yet many millennials' attributes were a function of age, and will change as they grow older. Hippies are prime examples of this. I don't necessarily believe that hippies 'sold out' as much as they 'grew up' and began to deal with new realities including kids, mortgages, work, or running companies.

Our lives are shaped by the realities and limitations of our surroundings. I just read Theodore H. White's The Making Of The President[1] series, to see how even the most idealist candidate is quickly cut down to size by the office, just as the most freedom-loving hippie was eventually shaped by his or her office, be that procurement manager or vice president.

---

[1] http://www.amazon.com/Theodore-H.-White/e/B001IXU698

Over the last year or so, there has been numerous articles proclaiming how selling has changed; more specifically, that selling to millennials, or conversely the 'millennial as a buyer,' is and will be a different that selling to previous generations. This is absolutely true for consumer buyers, but is not for B2B.

My first sales manager was a hippie, and every bit 'The Man' whom he and his 'bros' [had once] protested against. As were many of the buyers I sold to, when it came to buying, forget the Sgt. Pepper's poster on the wall. They were much more like their fathers than John Lennon. It was clear from the report that many millennial attributes will change as this generation ages, including how they behave and buy when they have profit and loss accountability or for success of their company.

It's easy to understand why many people want to extend social tools on the consumer experience to B2B, especially given the millennials' appetite for all things social. But B2B sellers are just another consumer group, susceptible to the same marketing ploys as any other consumer groups. And it's why we should be a little suspicious of all the talk around this generation being different.

There's no denying that tools and apps available today change the mechanics of how people sell and buyers' access to information. These new devices certainly have a positive impact on how we sell, but they don't change why people buy, be they millennials or any other demographic. B2B selling is about how we can help B2B buyers achieve their economic objectives, which in turn are shaped by their 'office.' To confuse tangible economic outcome with the means of delivery is risky, and frankly, no different than making the same mistakes others have made in the past. Good selling is not about the tools, or latest gadgets. A fool with a tool is still a fool.

Being a 1957 Cynic, I'm sensitive to the world 'different,' and every time I'm told things are different, I remember all the prior 'differents' I've encountered: the October 1987 market slide, the S&L crisis, the Dotcom boom and bust, the housing bubble of the mid-2000s, the subprime crisis, subsequent market meltdown and run up that follows. All different.

I bet Theodore White turned over when we were told Obama was going to be different. My hippie customers were not different, nor is your Gen X. Do you really think the millennial buyer will be?

About the Author

Tibor Shanto – Principal, <u>Renbor Sales Solutions Inc.</u>

Tibor Shanto has been a sales leader for over 25 years, helping companies achieve and improve their revenue goals. Initially as a sales rep, then progressing to leadership roles with companies including Globe and Mail, Dow Jones, Factiva and Reuters. Tibor has been called a brilliant sales tactician, helping sales teams and organizations to better execute their sales process. As a principal with Renbor Sales Solutions, working with leading B2B sales organizations improving critical aspects of their sales cycle, including shorten sales cycles, increase close ratios, and create double digit growth through the execution of their strategy by using the right combination of strategic and tactical execution supported by metrics and our Follow-Through Action Plan.

Tibor works with <u>leading companies</u>[1], helping them achieve <u>sustained behavioral change and success</u>[2], leading them to say: "<u>We look forward to an ongoing relationship with Tibor, who for my money is Canada's number one sales trainer.</u>"[3]

Tibor co-authored the award winning book <u>Shift!: Harness The Trigger Events That Turn Prospects Into Customers</u>[1], (see below), and contributor to Office Technology magazine, The Huffington Post, Globe and Mail Report on Small Business, Today's Trucking, has appeared on Business News Network, CHCH-TV, and others.

Tibor Shanto
+1 416 822-7781
(855) 25-SALES
Tibor.Shanto@SellBetter.ca
<u>www.SellBetter.ca</u>

---

[1] http://www.sellbetter.ca/clients/
[2] http://www.sellbetter.ca/clients/case-studies/
[3] http://www.sellbetter.ca/testimonials/
[1] http://www.amazon.com/Tibor-Shanto/e/B0043TEI84/ref=ntt_athr_dp_pel_pop_2

 http://www.SellBetter.ca/Blog

@TiborShanto

ca.linkedin.com/in/tiborshanto/

www.youtube.com/sellbetter

www.facebook.com/Renbor.Sellbetter

gplus.to/TiborShanto

Awards and Recognition:

Ranked 8th on the Top 30 Social Salespeople In The World – Forbes.com 2014
Top 50 Sales & Marketing Influencers for 2015 – Top Sales World
50 Most Influential People in Sales Lead Management in 2014
Gold Medal Top Sales & Marketing Blog 2013 – Top Sales World Awards
Top 50 Sales & Marketing Influencers for 2014 – Top Sales World
Top 25 Sales Influencers for 2014– OpenView Labs
50 Most Influential People in Sales Lead Management in 2013
Top 50 Sales & Marketing Influencers for 2013 – Top Sales World
Top 25 Sales Influencers for 2013– OpenView Labs
Top 50 Sales & Marketing Blogs 2012 – Top Sales World
25 Influential Leaders In Sales – 2012 Edition – InsideView
Top 50 Sales & Marketing Influencers for 2012 – Top Sales World
Top 25 Sales Influencers for 2012 – OpenView Labs

Book time with Tibor by going to:
Http://tiborshanto.youcanbook.me

www.ingramcontent.com/pod-product-compliance
Lightning Source LLC
Chambersburg PA
CBHW080611180526
45168CB00007B/2865